FLATLINERS

A GUIDE TO PRAIRIE LIVING

BY JASON HOWELL

CARTOONS BY PETE McCULLOUGH

Jason How

PERMANENT PRESS

FLATLINERS: A GUIDE TO PRAIRIE LIVING

Copyright © 1998 by Jason Howell

ISBN: 0-9682972-1-8

Printed by Hignell Book Printing

Published in Manitoba by Permanent Press

Collector's edition.

DEDICATION

Dedicated to everyone who has been left behind on the prairies. And to those who abandoned us, many thanks for leaving food and not putting us down.

This book is also dedicated to the Federal Government, for keeping us barefoot and pregnant, even though I still say they shouldn't be sleeping with our women.

ACKNOWLEDGEMENTS

Thanks to the many people whose jokes and stories I remember, but whose names I don't. To Shannon Howell and Kris Cowley, for their editing advice. And finally, to Aunt Judy, for being there when we needed her the most.

CONTENTS

INTRODUCTION

It is my hope, dear reader, that this book about the joys of prairie living will, at the very least, find a place in each and every outhouse on the prairies. I also hope that it will stand the test of time . . . as well as all those flies and stuff. This is not, after all, just another book of jokes that fall flat--no, this one's got pictures, too. Yes, its got pictures and, as far as I can tell, it is the very first prairie cartoon book ever published. So give it an important spot in your biffy, would you?

From a very young age I thought I had a book in me. Turns out it was just a piece of undigested sandwich, but it still inspired me (the thought, not the sandwich) to write this book. Why write about the prairies? Because it's a funny place to live. I don't think anyone would argue with that. We're either struggling with the elements to stay alive, or we're so bored we can't even look alive. But, through it all, prairie people have always been able to laugh at everything --including themselves. Hopefully, this book provides something more to laugh at, but, if not, as an added bonus, it makes excellent fertilizer.

SECTION #1

SIGHTSEEING ON THE PRAIRIES

IT'S A SMALL WONDER
TOWN

Maybe you've walked along the Great Wall of China, explored the mysteries of Egypt's pyramids, or seen the ruins of the Parthenon in Greece. Wherever your travels have taken you, and whatever you've seen before, nothing will have prepared you for this. Welcome to the Western Canadian Prairies and our tour of Small Town Wonders. For years people have driven past these sites and monuments and wondered, "What the hell's up with that?" Now, in what is sure to be turned into some 8-hour A&E mini-series, I have uncovered the secret origins of these monuments. I expect that, when the full story is revealed, flocks of tourists will be jam-packed on the #1 Highway, waiting to pay homage to these shrines. In the interest of preserving life as it is for the locals (without the use of formaldehyde), Prairie Tourism has asked that you refrain from bringing any "trappings of civilization."

MIDDLE OF NOWHERE STRAIGHT AHEAD

WELCOME TO ALBERTA . . .

PROUD OF OUR RAT-FREE HERITAGE.

Welcome to Alberta . . .

- one more word about how intolerant we are, and we'll kick your minority ass.

- we've had oil and we've had gas. Oil is better.

- consider Banff as much your's as it is our's. That is to say, consider it Japan's.

- home of the "ten-gallon head."

- we fully support bilingualism--English and "Albertan."

- where vegetarians still don't have the right to vote.

Welcome to Glendon, AB . . .

Home of the World's Largest Perogy

The "perogy choice," as it will be remembered forever, was one of the most difficult decisions in the history of Glendon. Many residents voted for head cheese to be the town monument, and still more took up the cause of farmer's sausage. The mayor at that time, however, won the town over with the argument that the perogy was able to incorporate both meat and cheese and was therefore superior. The debate didn't end there, however, as 13 people were injured in a riot over whether the perogy was better boiled or fried.

Welcome to St. Paul, AB . . .
Home of the World's First UFO Landing Pad

 Around the time St. Paul was founded, people reported seeing mysterious men in black on several occasions. After each sighting, a new crop circle was discovered. The locals, convinced that the time of first contact was at hand, built a landing pad to attract aliens. It was only years later that they discovered the real cause of the crop circles-- Hutterites who'd come into town to test drive the new John Deeres. Some still claim it was aliens, though, who ended up in Ottawa and have been runnin' the country ever since.

Welcome to Vegreville, AB . . .
Home of the World's Largest Easter Egg

Desperate to escape "the Old Country," and all those stories that inevitably come with it, the original Vegrevillians hatched an elaborate escape plan. They created this giant egg, hid inside it, and had themselves shipped to Alberta. Unfortunately, they arrived in mid-January and they all froze to death. Their courage was an inspiration to others, though, who, scratching "The Egg Plan" from their list, simply took the next available boat.

Welcome to Vilna, AB . . .
Home of the World's Largest Mushrooms

After a lengthy RCMP investigation, an entire town was thrown in jail in the biggest mushroom bust in prairie history. Accustomed to the normal call-ins about pink elephants, police began receiving new reports of 20 foot high mushrooms. After crawling down a hole and chasing a gopher with a timepiece, police came across a huge "Eat Me" sign. As it turns out, this was not the town slogan but a reference to the mushrooms. All charges have since been dropped, but the town has been asked to move to BC.

WELCOME TO SASKATCHEWAN...

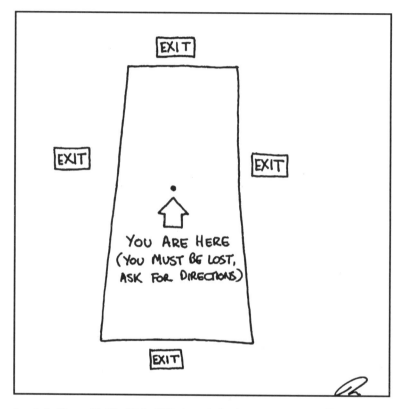

LAND OF THE LIVING SKIES...
HOME OF THE LIVING DEAD

Welcome to Saskatchewan . . .

- . . . we're closed

- where everything you see can be explained by our own version of Einstein's Theory of Relativity--everyone's a relative.

- we're the folks those pro-lifers don't want you to see.

- where if you order a lap dance, you'll get a friendly pomeranian.

- we don't give a damn about Daylight Savings --and we're 20 years behind because of it.

- wait, don't go . . . we just got canned pop!

Welcome to Churchbridge, SK . . .
Home of the World's Largest Dollar Coin

A few years back, rumour has it, the entire town was addicted to VLTs. It got so bad that newborns were being named Orange, Cherry and Lucky 7. The town went into rehab, not a second too soon, and decided to melt down all their coin to stand as a constant reminder of their former addiction. The trouble is, the town is now divided on how to spend this oversized loonie, and have put off making a decision until their next major project is completed--the World's Largest VLT Machine.

Welcome to Langenburg, SK . . .

Home of Gopherville

Gopherville, the Disney World of Highway #16, has breathtaking attractions like the World's Tallest Bicycle and the Land of Miniatures. Every year, people from all over the world drive past it. Officially ranked by Prairie Tourism as one of the 7 circles of Hell, Gopherville is free to get in, but does charge a very reasonable $8.50 to get out.

Welcome to Porcupine Plain, SK . . .
Home of Quilly Willy

Love on the prairies is sort of like a porcupine . . . don't you think? I'm not sure how. I guess it's more like two porcupines . . . in that it's hard to get close to someone. Maybe it's because prairie men only allow themselves to feel love from a distance. I think that's what the town meant when they erected Quilly Willy. Either that or maybe it was a tribute to some guy who, from the sounds of it, must have been a real prick.

Welcome to Watson, SK . . .
Home of Santa Claus

Once upon a time, every province had their own North Pole and Santa. The kids were happier, the elderly didn't complain as much, blah, blah, blah. Then came the evil age of downsizing, and the decision, based on cost-efficiency, to have one North Pole and one Santa serving the entire country. Ever since then, no one answers the letters, the kids don't get what they want, and my pants don't fit. As for the Watson Santa, since he was laid off, he hasn't budged from that spot. . . but people bring him food and stuff so he's OK.

WELCOME TO MANITOBA . . .

WHERE WINTER DRIVING QUALIFIES AS AN EXTREME SPORT.

Welcome to Manitoba . . .

- if you are reading this, you hereby waive the right to take legal action, should you, at some point during your trip, freeze your ass off.

- we were retro when retro wasn't cool.

- E I E I O--we'll put our knowledge of the alphabet up against anyone's.

- where the burning philosophical question is not "Who am I?" but "Why am I here?"

- . . . and on your left, you'll see . . . sorry, there's nothing there. On your right, there's a . . . You know what? Just keep driving.

Welcome to Gladstone, MB . . .
Home of Happy Rock

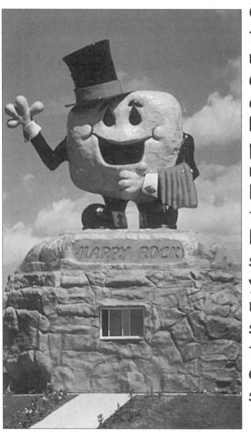

Originally called Gallstone, the town was named after an early mayor who passed a stone after CN pulled out. When the town didn't die, however, the stone became a good luck charm, and people came from all over to rub it and wish for a good harvest. As part of the ritual, they would dance around holding their stomachs, screaming out obscenities and yelling, "My gallstone . . . it's my %!@%* gallstone . . . won't somebody help me?" Just off the #1, Gladstone is minutes away from another tourist hot spot, Bleeding Ulcer, MB.

Welcome to Dauphin, MB . . .
Home of Giardia Beaverus

The truth is finally out. By day, the giant beaver stood guard over the people of Dauphin. By night, he was urinating in the town's water supply. . . even in Dauphin this is not acceptable. The town is convinced that this act of hostility, performed by Canada's symbol, was no accident. They see it as the direct consequence of liberal tendencies on Parliament Hill, and, unless they receive an apology, have vowed to bring this country to its knees (next time, they'll vote Conservative).

Welcome to Boissevain, MB . . .
Home of Tommy the Turtle

Boissevain – HOME OF **CANADIAN** TURTLE DERBY

Tommy carried the burden of low self-esteem with him wherever he went. Then, one day a visitor saw Tommy at the annual Turtle Derby and commented on his size. No one in town ever thought of him as anything but funny-looking, but now they saw him as a huge tourist attraction. Tommy's ego soared as people flocked to Boissevain and actually paid money to see him. Unfortunately, one weekend everyone went into the city and forgot to feed him and, well, let's just say business has been pretty slow ever since.

Welcome to Winnipeg, MB . . .
Home of the Golden Boy

The Golden Boy stands as an inspiration to poor, naked farm boys across the province. He represents, not, as you might think, the burning desire to light your barn on fire and claim the insurance--no, he represents the enterprising spirit of our forefathers. Years ago, farmers would drive into Winnipeg just to go to the legislative building. And by the light of a torch, 240 feet up, they could see clear across the border...just far enough to see places where they could unload their wheat for a better price.

SECTION 2
PRAIRIE MIGRATION

WAS IT SOMETHING WE SAID ? ? ?

Despite small town wonders like The World's Largest Perogy and Happy Rock, prairie tourism numbers are still way down. In fact, not only is tourism suffering, but some residents are actually leaving. Why? Well, we can't say it's part of the general "brain drain" that is affecting the rest of Canada, as plenty of dumb people are leaving as well. The provincial governments in the West, concerned for our economic future, commissioned a study that would analyse this migration. Tracking devices were implanted in pieces of beef jerky (sold at fine gas stations everywhere) to monitor the mass exodus of people. Although the final results of the study are not yet in--as no one has ever actually come back--some findings have been reported. Over 50% of the beef jerky ended up in Toronto, perhaps because farmers thought that any place named "Hogtown" surely would give them better prices for their pigs. Most of the rest wound up in Vancouver, proving the attraction of a lucrative squeegee career. And if you too, dear reader, are thinking of leaving the prairies, just remember--"Things are pretty much the shits all over."

MOVING TO TORONTO

IF YOU'RE MOVING TO TORONTO . . .

YOU'VE GOTTA REALLY WANT THE CHEESE.

IF YOU'RE MOVING TO TORONTO . . .

THE **401** IS A GREAT PLACE TO RAISE YOUR KIDS.

IF YOU'RE MOVING TO TORONTO . . .

YOU'LL SEE THE BEST PRO SPORTS HAS TO OFFER.

IF YOU'RE MOVING TO TORONTO . . .

YOU'RE NO LONGER A BIG FISH IN A SMALL POND--
YOU'RE A SARDINE.

MOVING TO VANCOUVER

IF YOU'RE MOVING TO VANCOUVER . . .

CONGRATULATIONS! BEING A HOMELESS PERSON HAS NEVER BEEN MORE EXCITING.

IF YOU'RE MOVING TO VANCOUVER . . .

DON'T FORGET TO BRAG ABOUT THE WEATHER . . .
LIKE WE DON'T GET RAIN.

IF YOU'RE MOVING TO VANCOUVER . . .

TRY TO GET A CLOSET WITH AN OCEAN-SIDE VIEW.

THERE'S NO SUCH THING AS A BAD REASON TO SMOKE POT.

EL NINO WAS A PRAIRIE BOY . . .

You've gotta be tough to live on the prairies. Out here, we get four seasons of the year like anywhere else, it's just that they come in no particular order. It's not like in Vancouver, where if they get 2 inches of snow the city shuts down and the phone lines are jammed with everyone trying to call their mommies. Do you remember that El Nino guy? The truth is, he actually grew up in rural Manitoba, and I can remember we used to make fun of him. He wasn't tough at all. Even the girls used to kick his ass. The day after he spilled some water in Manitoba, the newspaper headline read, "YOU CALL THAT A FLOOD?" El Nino retired soon after, moving to the coast to live with his big sissy friends. But I hope his erratic behaviour continues, even in retirement. . . I really do. Maybe, we'll end up exchanging weather with Vancouver, and then, for once, we'd get the last laugh.

PRAIRIE WINTERS GET SO COLD . . .

EVEN THEM HOOKERS WEAR SNOWSUITS.

THE **#1** CAUSE OF ALL PRAIRIE DIVORCES IS FAILURE TO AGREE ON THE THERMOSTAT SETTING. BE PREPARED TO COMPROMISE.

PRAIRIE WINTER SURVIVAL TIP #2

NEVER SET OUT IN A BLIZZARD WITH A
HORSE THAT CAN'T FIND ITS WAY HOME.

PRAIRIE WINTER SURVIVAL TIP **#3**

DON'T FORGET TO BEND YOUR KNEES
WHEN SHOVELLING SNOW.

A PRAIRIE SPRING COMES SUDDENLY . . .

AND ALWAYS PROMISES A CHANGE OF FORTUNE.

PRAIRIE SUMMERS ARE SO HOT . . .

YOU LOSE WHATEVER FINGERS AND TOES YOU'VE GOT
LEFT FROM WINTER TO SPONTANEOUS COMBUSTION.

PRAIRIE SUMMER SURVIVAL TIP #1

KEEP AN EYE ON THE OLDTIMERS. IF IT'S GONNA RAIN,
THEY CAN FEEL IT IN THEIR BONES.

PRAIRIE SUMMER SURVIVAL TIP #2

ACCEPT THE FACT THAT YOU'LL NEVER BE ABLE TO
"DRESS FOR THE WEATHER." IT CHANGES SO QUICKLY,
THAT YOU'LL ALWAYS BE 5 MINUTES TOO LATE.

EXPECT A BIG STORM IF . . .

- folks start saying "it looks like the best crop yet."

- them pigs and chickens get real extra quiet-like.

- you're a sitting duck out there in the old biffy, and the 100-yard dash never was your strong suit.

- someone asks why you turned the lights out, and you don't even have electricity.

- you live in a trailer park.

- you walk down main street and see more businesses with windows boarded up than usual.

- it's Saturday night . . . and the bingo hall is empty!

A PRAIRIE FALL IS SO COLD . . .

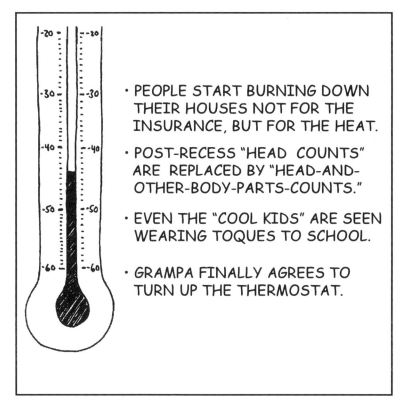

- PEOPLE START BURNING DOWN THEIR HOUSES NOT FOR THE INSURANCE, BUT FOR THE HEAT.

- POST-RECESS "HEAD COUNTS" ARE REPLACED BY "HEAD-AND-OTHER-BODY-PARTS-COUNTS."

- EVEN THE "COOL KIDS" ARE SEEN WEARING TOQUES TO SCHOOL.

- GRAMPA FINALLY AGREES TO TURN UP THE THERMOSTAT.

BUT IF YOU CARRY A RECTAL THERMOMETER WITH YOU, AT LEAST YOU'LL HAVE THE SATISFACTION OF KNOWING PRECISELY WHEN YOU FROZE YOUR ASS OFF.

SECTION 4

FLATLINING

(AND OTHER PRAIRIE HOBBIES)

THE SEARCH FOR SIGNS OF LIFE

Life on the prairies moves at a slow and leisurely pace. To outsiders, this slow pace can seem, well . . . just plain boring. What they don't realize is that all the really important stuff is going on inside our heads--like when we decide what we want for supper and stuff. Sure, it's not like in Toronto, where they waste all their time commuting to work or sitting in traffic jams. Here a person has more free time . . . and can choose to waste it on other things. I've always found a good hobby to be a very effective way to fritter away my existence. And, as an added bonus, I've actually learned stuff from my hobbies, too. Like, in high school, when we used to cruise up and down the main street of our small town, back and forth, up and down, I learned that I never, ever wanted to go back there again.

Probably the most popular hobby, an activity that will consume much time for little or no compensation, is farming. The following pages contain other harmless hobbies that, with a little attention, can turn into full-blown, life-consuming obsessions.

MODEL RAILROADING

HIGH STAKES GAMBLING

BIRD WATCHING

PAINTING THE TOWN RED

KILLING GOPHERS

ATTENDING FUNERALS

SUPPORTING LOST CAUSES

PLAYIN' COWBOY

SECTION 5
PRAIRIE AILMENTS
(& A FEW HOME REMEDIES)

THIS CHAPTER MAY SAVE YOUR LIFE . . .

In this day and age, doctors no longer make house calls. And, even if they still did, we all know they can't be trusted. They're always recommending needless surgeries and . . . organ transplants. No, we're better off without them. Instead, look around you, your fate rests in the hands of these people. Isn't that comforting? And with a little advice, you can overcome any ailments that come your way (or strike you down violently).

In general, the prairies provide the ideal environment to live a long and healthy life. Indeed, the slower pace of life and smog-free air have, no doubt, contributed to our distinction of having the most octogenarians (8-armed people) in the country. But sometimes even coffee and a muffin are not enough to keep people healthy. There are ailments unique to the prairies that everyone should know about. I'm not talking about anything exciting like Ebola or Flesh-Eating Disease, but there are others here that can make you equally dead. If you follow the suggested remedies for these ailments, this chapter may indeed save your life.

HYPOTHERMIA???

Turning blue . . . an even deeper blue than normal? If you've just been rescued after falling through ice, being lost in a blizzard, or leaving the house without your longjohns, there's a good chance you have hypothermia.

A LITTLE HYPOTHERMIA NEVER KILLED ANYONE

You probably just need some fresh air. Open a window, especially if it's mid-winter--or, better still, go down to the lake, cut a hole in the ice and do that polar-bear-club-thing. Note: although hypothermia never killed anyone, you can die from drowning, so be sure to wait at least half an hour after eating.

SIGNS OF SEVERE FROSTBITE

Most prairie doctors view the check-up as an opportunity to amputate before the gangrene sets in. Watch for these tell-tale signs that amputation is needed:

- your waiter compares the coloring of the blackened chicken to your fingers.

- the local gardening show awards First Prize for Best Cauliflowers to . . . your ears.

- everyone who passes you on the street seems to want to mark your limbs with an X.

- the nurse never mentions walking again, and instead is all gung-ho on this new roll-yourself-around-method.

- the doctor all of a sudden remarks, "Isn't it wonderful that people can replace fingers with their toes?"

MORE SIGNS OF SEVERE FROSTBITE

- you receive your first ever invitation to a War Amps meeting.

- the doctor refers to your upcoming operation as a "kind of circumcision for big boys."

- when you check into the hospital, instead of a wheelchair, they give you a skateboard and a cup.

- your kids play "This Little Piggy" with you, and in each case the piggy dies a horrible, horrible death.

- the hospital has an expiry date stamped on your toes.

- the wall chart refers to you as "Stumpy."

FARM ACCIDENT???

On every farm there is someone, usually an uncle, who feeds his arms or legs to a piece of hungry farm machinery. If this has just now happened to your uncle, don't panic. It is a common occurrence that no more requires a doctor than a stubbed toe or the common cold.

REATTACHING LIMBS FOR BEGINNERS

To reattach his limbs, you're going to need some strong binder twine. Run to the barn and get it now, while your uncle lies there and reads this book (holding it open with his teeth, if necessary). Now, place the arm/leg (be sure to get it right) in its proper position and tie it firmly to the stump. Then, find a milk-soaked piece of bread to lay on the wound to combat infection. Wrap the whole thing up with a strip of duct tape and, with any luck, he won't even miss a day's work.

EXTREMELY RED NECK???

Patients with this condition often don't realize they have it (being unable to see the back of their own necks). If you are concerned that you, too, might be a redneck (and if so, wish to qualify for your Alberta benefits), take the following true or false test.

_____ I drink at least a six-pack of beer daily.
_____ My pride and joy is my .22 collection.
_____ Beef jerky is one of the four major food groups.
_____ Archie Bunker was my role model.
_____ Minorities are lowering my property value.
_____ I sometimes receive mail addressed to "White Trash."
_____ The country is run on my personal tax dollar.

REFORM YOURSELF

If you scored 1 or more, you are an ideal candidate for the Reform Party. For more information, call 1-800-RED-NECK.

BLINDNESS???

If you see a blind person in need of assistance, check their pockets for a flask. After all, too much hooch can cause temporary blindness.

SEE THE LIGHT

If the subject seems to have been blind for more than a couple of days, and, most importantly, if he has a white cane and a dog with him, he may actually be blind, in which you case you can't help him and you probably shouldn't be searching through his pockets.

HORIZONTITIS?!?

Unable to see objects far away, in the upper half of your field of vision? You, like many other prairie people, have what is commonly known as horizontitis. Your gradual loss of sight is just your body's way of telling you, once and for all, that there's nothing out there worth seeing.

USE YOUR IMAGINATION

Imagination is essential on the prairies, that and a flask of good hooch (see section on blindness). Eventually, out of sheer boredom, let's be honest, your mind starts inventing elaborate adventures set against more beautiful landscapes. The world becomes a smashing Imax film of your own making, for your own personal screening. You spend most of your day jousting with JonDar, the fire-breathing thresher. That is, until your dad comes home and encourages a different form of time travel--knocking you clear into next week for neglecting your chores.

COVERED IN LOCUSTS???

Although many prairie farmers think nothing of waking up to a bed full of locusts, and are actually thankful to have diverted the little critters' attention from their crops, there can be a down side as well. Burning piles of locusts in your living room, believe it or not, will never get you on the cover of Better Homes and Gardens.

TAKE THE BIG STEP

To keep the locusts out of your home, then, I would suggest that you finally do it. Yes, it's time to replace those dirt floors in your house with wooden ones. It's a big step, I know. But the next thing you know, you'll be talking on the telephone, putting in electricity and getting rid of that covered wagon out back.

HEADACHE???

If your head hurts somewhat and, upon looking in the mirror, you find yourself staring at a big hoof print, there is a good possibility you have been kicked in the head by a horse. Sadly, many prairie men have been kicked like this, and because of it are unable to talk or, if able to talk, can't listen.

KNOW WHAT'S GOOD FOR YOU

Throw out the aspirin. You just need to balance out your prairie Ying and Yang. What you need is another swift kick in the head--this time on the other side. Note: it is a good idea to tie yourself down in the stable first, just in case, at the last minute, you forget what's good for you.

DEPRESSION???

Life on the prairies has the rhythm of a song--unfortunately, it's a country song. You know . . . the one where your husband up and leaves you for a farm animal, and then your dog dies but the ground is too frozen to bury him so you and your six kids spend most of the winter just staring at his cold, rotting carcass, waiting for the bank to come and repossess your home.

BE MORE POSITIVE

When you're feeling down, just remember the power of positive thinking. You choose to see the glass as 1/2 empty or 1/2 full . . . of course, there's always an outside chance that it could be 1/2 frozen.

SPEECH DISORDERS???

Ever wonder why, even after millions of dollars have been spent on speech therapists, most of our kids still have speech problems? It's because these kids spend every winter recess hanging from the monkey bars by their tongues.

TEAR DOWN THOSE MONKEY BARS

Forget about Diana's lightweight land mine issue--do you see any land mines in your back yard? I didn't think so. Sign this petition to ban monkey bars from every school, and put them back in the zoo where they belong.

I, _____, *being of legal age to drink moonshine and have sex (after marriage), and being of sound mind, though not so sound as to move, do, as much as I do anything, hereby declare that them there monkey bar things should be banned.*

X _____   *Date* _____   *Witness* _____

Now rip this page out and fire it off to your local MP. They'll be impressed with your civic-mindedness.

GOPHER ANKLES???

For years prairie people have been twisting or breaking their ankles in gopher holes. And we sure haven't been very successful at killing the little devils, either. Now, after all these years, evolution has been kind enough to offer a solution. Children these days are being born with ankles so flexible that they can walk (or skate) on them.

DO THE PRAIRIE WALK

Scientists have found that people born with "gopher ankles," far from needing to be "cured," are actually better adapted to their environment. By walking on their ankles in a sliding motion, not only can they walk right over gopher holes, but they are also less prone to fall on ice. And, like seals, they can clap their feet on the ground to warn others of danger (oncoming tractors, etc.). Indeed, it is now being said that people with gopher ankles will be the "farm-hands" of the future.

SECTION 6
EVERYTHING YOU NEED TO KNOW ABOUT CURLING
(THE SPORT OF THE PRAIRIES)

A TEN-STEP CURLING PROGRAM

If you want to fit in with the "prairie crowd," you've gotta learn how to curl. The following ten-step program makes learning to curl painless (so painless, in fact, that you may actually experience a loss of all bodily sensation). It is hoped that, at the end of this section, if you haven't learned everything about curling, at least you'll be able to "bonspiel with confidence."

TAKE THE PLEDGE

I, _____, do hereby pledge to devote all my time (or at least my weekends)--to the detriment of my liver and against all better judgement--to sweeping the local rink's ice 'til it's good and clean.

SIGN THE WAIVER

Oh, yeah, and I also absolve the rink of all responsibility should it later prove that I did not meet the minimum age for curling, was allergic to alcohol or pretzels, or was fired for missing too many Mondays after weekend bonspiels.

X _____ Witness _____ Date __/__/__

STEP #1

<u>KNOW YOUR EQUIPMENT</u>

If you are a beginner to the sport of curling, you may be surprised at the kind of equipment you need:

- Beer (BYOT--bring your own two-four)

- Rye and Coke (the Gatoraid of curling)

- Corkscrews (for those curlers from out of town)

- Food (to help the beer go down)

- Brooms (to help you stand up)

- Head gear (permitting a more gentle passing out)

- Alarm clock (unless you want to miss last call)

STEP #2

LEARN THE CURLING JARGON

Biter	....	an ugly mixed bonspiel partner
Bonspiel	....	Octoberfest with brooms
Counter	....	where beer is served
End	....	time for a beer
Guard	....	rink security
Head	....	a BC curler
House	....	someone else is buying tonight
Nipple	....	center of the house
Rock	....	ice cube served in drinks
Runner	....	"Beer Runner" or "Offsale Boy"
Second	....	keeps duelling pistol for lead
Skip	....	skipper if the team ever goes sailing
Sticking	....	what your feet do in an arena washroom
Weight	....	time to switch to light beer?
Wobbler	....	a curler walking in a zig-zag motion

STEP #3

<u>CHECK YOUR PHYSICAL FITNESS (AT THE DOOR)</u>

Curling can be very demanding on an athlete's body--particularly their liver. Many a critical game has been lost because of the infamous "wussy liver." To prepare your liver properly, you need to simulate game conditions. Oldtimers suggest marinating your liver in ice cold beer for an entire weekend, stopping only to sweep the kitchen floor and slide yesterday's empties down your apartment hallway. It is also critical that you maintain a strict diet--eating nothing but pretzels or party mix. You should begin to see the results right away. When you look in the mirror, after adhering to such a strict training regimen, you might not recognize the unshaven, jaundiced, beer-bellied Briar challenger staring back at you.

STEP #4

LEARN THE RINK LAYOUT

The layout of most curling rinks is the same: you've got your ice, and you've got your bar area overlooking the ice. If you ever manage, through some huge oversight, to confuse the two, you may wind up curling. You don't want that. To make sure that never happens, when you enter a rink walk quickly, with eyes lowered, to the bar. Then, ignoring anyone who tries to start a conversation (especially if they begin with, "In the old country . . ."), order 3 or 4 drinks immediately. If, as often happens at bonspiels, someone doesn't show up or shows up but can't finish, there isn't a skip around who would even dream of taking you away from so many drinks.

STEP #5

DELIVERY AND RELEASE

If after your tenth "fruity drink," you find yourself, not unlike Sampson, holding up the washroom walls with every ounce of strength left in your body, dig your heels in the floor (use spurs if you have them) to create your own hack. Having established a more secure footing, launch yourself in the direction of the nearest game. Then, if this game seems to be moving at anything more than a snail's pace, you're still in trouble. You may need to "clear the house." To conceal your inebriated state, just in case some teetotalers are present, simply let yourself fall to the floor, keeping one arm raised (broom in hand). To maintain this "lights out" position for an extended period of time is, as in yoga, the mark of a great athlete. And don't worry, rink maintenance staff have been trained not to disturb curlers once they have entered "the zone," and will betray no signs of surprise should they see you still there in the morning.

STEP #6

<u>EXECUTING AN OUT-TURN</u>

You won't get very far in curling if you can't master the out-turn. "What's an out-turn?" you ask. The correct move involves holding a beer bottle at a 45-degree angle and, with a 1/4 turn of the wrist, twisting off the cap with your other hand. Torontonians, it is true, turn the bottle and hold the cap. It is unnecessary to learn the in-turn manoeuvre, as out West there is probably a law prohibiting any attempt at putting caps back on the bottles (and if there isn't, there should be). See illustration below for the all-important difference between the twist off and non twist off cap.

twist off

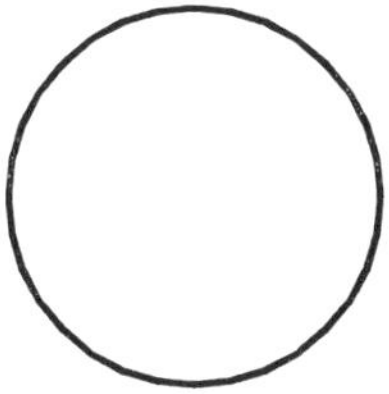

non twist off

STEP #7

FORGET ABOUT HOCKEY

One of the biggest "rookie mistakes" is to think of curling as a sport and compare it with hockey. The following chart illustrates the differences:

HOCKEY	CURLING
• losers beat up winners	• losers buy winners drinks
• shooting % is key statistic	• blood-alcohol % is key
• try to keep puck out of net	• try to keep self out of jail
• drug of choice: steroids	• drug of choice: Viagra
• drink beer after practise	• drinking beer is practise

STEP #8

GETTING IN THE HOUSE

Many curlers find that the mental strain of curling renders them incapable of driving home. In fact, walking home is not even an option, as they are often stricken with an inability to remember the particulars of their existence. They must rely on teamwork, then, to get each other home. When reminded who she is and where she lives, the lead will release herself in the general direction of her "house," relying on the curvature of the earth and the shortness of one of her legs to spin her in such a way as to land her right on her doorstep. It is the job of the other players to sweep the street in front of the lead, knowing full well that any tiny rock or piece of ice (real or imagined) may send her careening into the nearest snowbank. This pattern continues until the skip gets home, at which time everyone needs to get up again to be on time for the next game.

STEP #9

ADMITTING THAT YOU CURL

As with everything in life, as soon as you start to enjoy yourself people will talk. They'll say you have a problem--in this case, a "curling problem." They'll point to your 2 or 3 week's "sick time" for proof, showing that they have nothing better to do than count the days you're busy "practising." Though I would not put it on a job application, it is important to be open about your need to curl. If people suggest you need help, go to CAA or AAA, or wherever it is they send you, and admit that you curl. After all . . . it's the first step towards meeting someone else who does, too.

STEP #10

<u>GET A NICKNAME</u>

Congratulations! You've made it through our 10-step curling program. You are now, officially, a prairie curler. The only thing you need is a nickname. All the great players have one. Choose one from the list below that fits your personal style.

The Favoured Seed...K-Tel Record Holder...Canola Man.... The Widow Maker....Eric von Spieler...Heartbreaker.... Molson Man....Flash in the Bed Pan....The Big Question Mark Caesar....Momma's Boy....The Loose Canon....The 5th Tit Tinkerbell....Boozehound....The Last Choice....Dead Weight Hooch and Screech....The Place Holder....Ice Pick....Rattled Weeble Wobble ....The Magic Broom....The Letch....Jailbaiter The Slipping Clutch....Mr. Slip and Fall....Mr. Big End.......... The Gossip ....The Bad Ass....The Bottom Feeder....Mr.Freeze The Rainmaker....Sledgehammer....Air Rock....The Ice Man The Curler Formerly Known As Bob Smith....Sharon............

SECTION 7
PROFITABLE PRAIRIE OCCUPATIONS

BAREFOOT AND PREGNANT . . .

You know how, when it comes to job creation, people sometimes say that Ottawa keeps the prairies "barefoot and pregnant?" That's always bothered me. I mean, what's Ottawa doing sleeping with our women? Haven't they taken enough from us already? But, you know, for years we've been getting the bull, so I guess it's only natural that we get the horns, too. I'd really like to see Ottawa take its hands off prairie women, though, and start trying to attract more large companies to set up shop here. Oh, I realize that people would actually have to move here, but maybe the company could present the move to its employees as a natural extension of that "casual-Friday-thing."

Even without the government's help, you can still make a great living on the prairie. Think of this section as your career day, or--if "that farming thing" doesn't work out --your second career day.

GENERAL STORE OWNER

YOU'LL NEVER FIND A BETTER FORM OF TAX EVASION.

INDIAN GUIDE

REVIVE THE TIME-HONORED ROLE OF INDIAN GUIDE.
SO WHAT IF YOU'RE JUST A FAT, WHITE GUY LIVING
IN THE CITY. GREY OWL DID IT, AND SO CAN YOU.

FAMILY TREE HISTORIAN

A LAZY PERSON'S PATH TO RICHES.

CREATIVE FUNERAL PLANNER

BRING NEW VIGOUR AND EXCITEMENT TO THE IDEA OF DEATH. OUT ON THE PRAIRIES, THEY'LL PROBABLY WELCOME IT.

MANURE SALESMAN

PEOPLE SPEND A GREAT DEAL OF TIME EITHER SHOOTING IT OR DISTURBING IT. THEY'VE GOT TO BE GETTIN' IT FROM SOMEBODY.

MEDIA CELEBRITY

HOG PRICE ANALYST = CHICK MAGNET

MARKET GARDENER

GARDENING OFFERS THE UNIQUE OPPORTUNITY TO WORK HARDER IN YOUR RETIREMENT THAN YOU EVER DID IN YOUR WHOLE LIFE.

BEER BOTTLE COLLECTOR

ACCORDING TO FINANCIAL EXPERTS, MOST OF THE MONEY ON THE PRAIRIES IS NOT SITTING IN BANKS EARNING INTEREST--IT'S LYING IN COUNTRY DITCHES. THE ACT OF THROWING BEER BOTTLES FROM CAR WINDOWS IS PART OF AN AGE-OLD WESTERN TRADITION CALLED "PISSING AWAY YOUR INHERITANCE."

MINISTER

YOU MIGHT AS WELL BECOME A PREACHER--
EVERYTHING'S CLOSED ON SUNDAYS ANYWAY.

LOTTERY WINNER

AT LEAST THEN YOU COULD KEEP FARMING . . .
UNTIL ALL THE MONEY RAN OUT.

SECTION 8
PRAIRIE RELATIONSHIPS
(OR "HOW TO MARRY A RICH FARMER")

FOR REALLY FRUSTRATED FEMALES ONLY

In case you haven't noticed, there's not a lot of people on the prairies. In fact, there's so few that if someone moves back to town, everyone gets together for the "changing-of-the-population-sign" ritual. So you can imagine how hard it is to find a good man . . . they're so rare their seed is listed on the Winnipeg Grain Exchange. Forget about how lonely it gets being by yourself, you need someone just to keep your feet warm at night. And we need the population boost, so get out there and do your part. If you follow these "country rules" to dating, you may not get married, but at least you might get some meaningless sex every now and again. So, head out to the country, leave the big city behind, and find yourself a rich farmer.

FRUSTRATED MALES
PROCEED DIRECTLY TO PAGE 104

IF YOU WANT TO MARRY A RICH FARMER . . .

WALK EVERYWHERE WITH PAILS OF WATER AND,
WHATEVER YOU DO, DON'T LOOK TIRED.

IF YOU WANT TO MARRY A RICH FARMER . . .

SAY "PARDON ME" EVERY FEW HOURS, JUST IN CASE
HE HAPPENED TO SPEAK AND YOU MISSED IT.

DEVELOP CHILD-BEARING HIPS.

IF YOU WANT TO MARRY A RICH FARMER . . .

START SPREADING RUMOURS ABOUT YOURSELF.

IF YOU WANT TO MARRY A RICH FARMER . . .

IT'S OFTEN THE ONES YOU'D LEAST EXPECT.

IF YOU WANT TO MARRY A RICH FARMER . . .

HANG OUT AT ROBIN'S.

IF YOU WANT TO MARRY A RICH FARMER . . .

TALK TO HIS BANKER FIRST.

IF YOU WANT TO MARRY A RICH FARMER . . .

NEVER STOP WISHING FOR A FAIRY-TALE ENDING.

SECTION 9
HEIFER LOVE
(FOR FRUSTRATED MALES ONLY)

IF YOU'RE IN LOVE WITH A HEIFER . . .

SHOW HER THAT CHIVALRY IS ALIVE
AND WELL ON THE PRAIRIES.

IF YOU'RE IN LOVE WITH A HEIFER . . .

YOU'LL NEED A SLICK PICK UP LINE, COWPOKE.

IF YOU'RE IN LOVE WITH A HEIFER . . .

BRING FLOWERS ON THE FIRST DATE.

IF YOU'RE IN LOVE WITH A HEIFER . . .

TAKE HER TO A CLASSY RESTAURANT.

IF YOU'RE IN LOVE WITH A HEIFER . . .

DOUBLE-DATING USUALLY BREAKS THE ICE.

IF YOU'RE IN LOVE WITH A HEIFER . . .

TRY TO ACT LIKE YOU'RE MORE THAN JUST
"HORTI-CULTURED."

IF YOU'RE IN LOVE WITH A HEIFER . . .

JUST REMEMBER: FIRST KISS--NO TONGUE.

IF YOU'RE IN LOVE WITH A HEIFER . . .

KEEP THE RELATIONSHIP FRESH BY STAYING
OPEN TO NEW IDEAS

IF YOU'RE IN LOVE WITH A HEIFER . . .

EVENTUALLY YOU'RE GOING TO HAVE TO
MEET HER OLD MAN.

DISCLAIMER

At the advice of my lawyer, I wish to state that the previous section in no way intends to condone or encourage the improper usage of farm animals--even if they are consenting. Such behaviour is not common practise, despite what the statistics say, and does not set a good example for our young people. It is also critical to point out that at no time did the cartoon farm-hand and the heifer ever engage in real (or cartoon) sex. As a matter of fact, they are just close friends. Any opinion to the contrary would involve, as in the case of Bill Clinton, a serious misrepresentation of the facts.

SECONDARY DISCLAIMER

In the above disclaimer, in no way did I mean to imply that Mr. Clinton, by his presence in that context, was having sex with farm animals or, for that matter, anything but young interns.

Before you leave, just remember:

PRAIRIE FLAT HAS ITS ADVANTAGES . . .

- your dog can run away and 3 days later you can still enjoy seeing him run . . . but not have to scoop up after him.

- there's less roll back from driving a standard.

- you feel a sense of equality when you live on the "flood plain"--everyone has an equal chance of getting flooded.

- except for the snow, the prairies are a tourist mecca for wheelchair users.

- glacier advances will be that much easier the second time 'round.

- because there are no mountains around, "it's not there." And because "it's not there," we don't have to do it.

ABOUT THE AUTHOR

Author Jason Howell's first book, "101 Uses for an Old Sandbag" (Permanent Press, 1997), was a Winnipeg Free Press #1 best-seller. Howell grew up in Alberta and Manitoba, and spent some time later, after a prison transfer, in Saskatchewan. As a prairie kid, his favourite hobbies were collecting beer bottles and staring down at his shoes.   He was a little slow, by all accounts, and did not speak a word until the age of 28. He is currently working on more regional humour titles, and will get his mom to call you when they come out.

ABOUT THE ILLUSTRATOR

Freelance cartoonist Pete McCullough, co-creator of "that sandbag book," lives in Winnipeg and spends much of his time researching his material in bars and seedy pool halls. That's really all I know about the guy.